MY LAWN IS DRIVING ME CRAZY!

By

ROBERT VINCENT SIMS
"THE GARDEN REBEL"

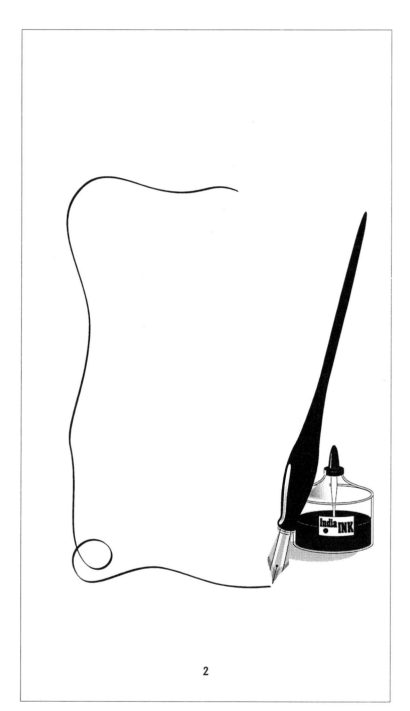

INTRODUCTION

The quest for a beautiful lawn just may be the most challenging aspect of gardening. Growers, all over the world, want to be proud of their lawns. Whether your lawn is minimal, in a zero lot line development, or whether it's over five acres on a sprawling hilltop estate doesn't really matter. All that matters is that it looks as good as it possibly can for as long as it possibly can.

As a landscape designer I know that it is critical for a lawn to look its best because it's the total picture that helps create the theme. Regardless of how perfect the trees are or how dramatic the shrub beds are the theme is incomplete without a good-looking lawn.

Besides aesthetics, lawns can be quite functional for recreational purposes. I've always thought it important to provide as large of an open area when possible so kids can put together a soccer game or families can put together grand outdoor events, if desired.

In my yard, I designed it to have a few trees in the front but most in the back. The house sits on a hill overlooking several gently rolling acres and I didn't want anything to restrict the view. The backyard was designed with many varieties of fruit, shade and nut trees and I placed and spaced them within the lawn.

Some trees are connected with large undulating islands of shrubs and groundcovers to help reduce the amount of lawn for lower maintenance. The important thing to remember is to always think long term and ask yourself, how does my family use this yard? I know in my particular case we enjoy sitting out on the lawn chairs to enjoy the day and to watch the birds flutter from tree to tree. We like to sit at various angles so that we can appreciate the open spaces as well as the lush island areas in the back surrounded by a thick beautiful lawn. My home office is designed so that I can open up the windows and sort of bring the outdoors in. I find it especially beautiful to see the sun spots under the trees on the lawn. Silhouetted branch patterns are mirrored on the grass creating fascinating shade patterns.

A good-looking landscape is rarely an instant thing, many yards evolve over many years. One thing will always remain constant - if the lawn isn't maintained, the rest of the yard as well as the house will take on that all familiar "last guy at the bar look." Staying on a regular maintenance schedule and heading off potential problems early will result in lawn success. Don't let anyone tell you it isn't work because it is. Like anything else that's worthwhile, big dividends will pay off. I'm a big believer in appreciating what you have by taking care of it. Your lawn and your landscape are your personal nests to make as beautiful as they can be. Regardless of how stunning a home's architecture may be, a house simply will not have the visual impact if the lawn is in poor shape. A good-looking lawn not only will make you feel great but it will help keep the property value up. Everyone needs to do their part to keep the neighborhood from going down hill. The homeowners' associations that are serious about maintaining property values give a lot of credence to beautiful lawns. It's a responsibility not only to yourself but also to your neighbors.

To maintain a green, lush lawn--the timing, in which you mow, feed, seed, and eliminate bugs and diseases, is critical. This timing I'm referring to is a commitment to nurture the lawn at the proper time. It is the timing that messes everybody up. Each person will give you a different answer. A good-looking yard is more of an art form than it is an exact science. This is because the conditions vary from yard to yard, day to day. Besides that, people differ in how nice a lawn they want. Some want it flawless, others just want to keep it alive and do the absolute minimal amount of work needed to get by. My main suggestion to you is to try your best to follow all the details of this book because the only thing tougher and more shocking than taking care of your existing lawn is buying a new one!

There is always plenty of work to do, but man, oh man, when you're done grab your ice tea and favorite lawn chair and relax. It will all be worth it.

Robert Vincent Sims

6

1

MASTER THE BASICS

Watering

The first thing is to be aware of any county or municipal water regulations. Depending on where you live, there may be specific times when you are legally able to water. We all share the same backyard, so to speak, so it's important to do our part when it comes to water conservation. Generally speaking, I think most people water too much anyway, and when the seasonal rains come, many forget to adjust their timers and the lawns stay too wet, helping to perpetuate a variety of problems.

The right amount of water for most varieties is critical for a lush dense turf, too much and the lawn diseases take over, too little and the grass can't maintain its existence. Bahia is the lawn grass that has the ability to withstand heavy drought and still regenerate. For most lawns if they are under stress from lack of water, it will eventually take its toll. We must remember that food manufactured by photosynthesis and important nutrients are absorbed by the roots and are then translocated to all parts of the plant. The temperatures of the plants are maintained by their transpiration of water. When it comes to seeds, without water they won't even germinate. In the summer as temperatures rise it's more important to keep a close eye on your watering schedule. The soil will determine how often a lawn needs watering. I know of people who live on lakes and have rich topsoil that looks like it came from an Iowa farm. They don't have sprinkler systems and they never have to water by hand, their soils simply hold enough moisture within their own microclimates, and their lawns look great. I know other people that have soils so sandy that if they're not watered every other day the lawns will actually wilt. For these lawns it's important to not neglect your fertilizing. Sandy soils leach quickly and the lawn always has a malnourished look. In dry, sandy soil you should also feed in smaller doses than you normally might, since any leaching is a waste of money and not environmentally sensitive. By feeding sandy lawns just what they can eat at any time you adjust or customize the feeding schedule for your lawn.

Amount of Water

I really want to simplify this area for you, and it's important for you to understand that each lawn has it's own specific personality and neighborhood in which it grows up. A lawn's personality is influenced by a variety of factors. There are various amounts of light and moisture in each and every lawn.
Nevertheless, I can offer you a basic guide that can be your starting point. For most lawns two or three times per week in the summer and once every week to two weeks in the winter will work fine. When you do water, you need to water with 3/4 to 1 inch of water each time as this will encourage deep roots. Deep roots are critical to develop over time as the lawn will hold up better in times of drought. During the winter season there is generally less rainfall which doesn't really end up hurting the grass because when it's dormant and not actively growing, it requires less water.

Over-watering promotes bugs, diseases, and weeds as well as wasting a much needed future resource. Maladjusted sprinklers can sometimes put more water on the sidewalk or street, which doesn't do your lawn any good. Get in the good habit of giving your lawn a weekly physical. While you're walking around early in the mornings with your coffee checking out the shrubs to see what's blooming don't forget to check the grass. Too much or too little water is guaranteed to cause problems in the future.

When to Water

1. If footprints or mower tire prints stay in the lawn.

2. When leaf blades are folded in half.

3. When soil from the root zone feels dry.

4. If lawn turns a blue grey or dull grey color.

5. If the lawn holds up an empty glass and asks you to fill it when you walk by.

The above symptoms occur when there are prolonged periods of drought, high temperatures and strong drying winds. Once the lawn shows signs of stress it is important to not procrastinate and water immediately.

Irrigation professionals now offer electronic rain gages that have special sensors which activate an automated timer to respond in times of drought. This is a handy device to have especially for people who go on vacation for over a week or for people who have seasonal homes. The good news is that by adding this convenience it simplifies your life and is not particularly expensive. There's no reason to delay, call your sprinkler professional today so that he can install it for you!

Time to Water

The best time to water is between 5:00 A.M. and 8:00 A.M. Watering should be finished when the sun starts to warm the earth as less evaporation results. Also, if you decide you want to pull weeds or do some shrub trimming early in the morning you don't want to be chased away by the sprinkler system. With most professional systems you'll need to water for at least 30-45 minutes to get a good deep root watering. Watering too lightly will not produce deep roots and too much is simply wasteful and can also perpetuate diseases. Thatch build-up is evidenced by lawns that stay too wet. Dollar weed, pennywort and sedge will often take over if kept too wet. As soon as you see even a few sprigs of weeds you need to take immediate action to eradicate. Once they reseed they thrive and will be much tougher to eliminate.

Sprinkler System Q.C.

QC is the Garden Rebel term that stands for quality check. I am astounded by the number of people who set their timers then never bother checking the individual heads. I suggest that you make a notation on your calendar to check the entire system once a month on a Saturday morning. That's right, get out there in your bathing suit and play in the water. You will be amazed what you find, such as heads not rotating in the proper direction, heads spraying on the sidewalk and driveway and sometimes a head that is stuck in one spot. Grains of sand or the impact from the mower tire can often be just enough to cause a problem. Sometimes a tiny piece of dried glue breaks off and clogs a sprinkler head.

Set up your sprinkler system so that the shrub beds and the lawn are on a separate zone. Grass does not grow as much in late fall and winter and consequently will not use as much water. Shady areas of the yard will not need as much water as sunny areas, if it stays too wet it encourages bugs and disease. **Remember to water deeply when you do water, as frequent light watering will help develop a shallow root system that will not hold up well in times of drought.**

Light is a Relative Term

There are really no grasses that love the shade. The operative word is tolerate. Shade is an interesting word because there are several gradations of shade. For example, dappled sunlight or sun spots evenly spaced under an open and well thinned oak is considered bright shade. Certain varieties do well under these conditions. Dense shade under trees with thick canopies that have not been thinned is almost certain death for grass. For these areas a groundcover will be the better choice.

Full all day open sun is what you need for the healthiest grass. Look how the pros do it, they grow it on sod farms in all day sun, not under thick trees! Since they make their living growing it I think they know best.

Sometimes people will tell me that a particular area of lawn is in full sun and they can't understand why the grass is dying. When I actually inspect the site, I often discover that it's in full sun all right, full morning sun for two hours. The rest of the day is total dense shade. For these hard to grow spots you better start thinking of a groundcover.

Don't throw money away. If the grass dies in the same spot after two replacements, then your yard is trying to tell you something. Grass is just not meant to grow everywhere!

Soil

Grass varieties can grow in a wide range of soils. The most important thing to remember is to have a soil that is well-drained. Any place that is low or where water puddles from run off, from a hill or driveway, is a problem waiting to expand. It is in these spots that bugs and diseases begin to rear their ugly heads. You may want to consider getting a soil test to determine the pH, which is the acidity or alkalinity of the soil. Certain species of grass prefer certain pH ranges. The pH is important because it determines the lawn's ability to supply nutrients to itself.

Soils that stay too wet can have a topsoil and sand mixture applied before planting so that no "wet" spots develop. Soils that are excessively dry can have cow manure and peat moss added to help hold moisture and nutrients longer around the roots, all of this should be done before planting.

Soils that are too compact won't be able to grow grass successfully. Adding more fertilizer or water will not solve the problem. Soils become compact because of their specific consistency or because of lawn mowers, vehicles, etc... over a long period of time going over the lawn. Good aeration is critical if the grass is to survive. If you have certain areas that continually die out due to compaction you will need to till this area and add extra organic matter to break it up. You may add cow manure, peat moss, small woodchips or perlite. Spend whatever time it takes to prevent any soil from becoming too compact because it will pay off in the long run. Once the soil is loosened a bit the roots of the grass will be able to develop deeper.

Should You get A Push Mower or A Rider?

It all depends on the size of your lawn. For me, since I've always had large yards I only ever considered riding mowers. It is important that you get the right size mower for your specific yard. If it's too large it may be harder for you to maneuver around the planting beds. I find cutting grass on a rider to be very relaxing. It's a great time to clear the mind fog and it's always been like a walk on the beach to me.

Different size mowers have different size tires. The tires are important because they determine the comfort of the ride and help in maneuverability. Riders tend to be very expensive but like anything else will usually last a long time if well taken care of.

One of the great features of a rider is

that a small utility trailer can usually be attached. This makes it very convenient to pick up small twigs and branches that fall. You can even haul compost around the yard and every spring and late summer the trailer will make it a lot easier for you to freshen up the mulch in the planting beds.

The Push Mower

If the yard is small or moderate in size a push mower is your best bet. I always felt that the self-propelled types were the only way to go as they glide through the grass with minimal effort.

I remember one particular landscape client of mine who specifically wanted a non-propelled mower because he said it was his only hour of exercise per week and he actually looked forward to it. For me, I would rather spend the time playing tennis, but hey, to each his own.

Take your time when buying a rotary mower. You will discover that there is a big price difference with various brands. I think the ones with all the bells and whistles tend to cost more and generally last longer. Buy one that has adjustable mowing heights so that you could cut through tall weeds or grass if you ever have to.

If you can't decide which mower to get then get the one that has a more powerful engine and a superior deck. Yes, you'll pay more but buy them in the late summer or early spring when the big sales are available.

The trailing shield is there for your protection as well as the protection of others. I'm aware that sometimes it can be irritating as it is in the way and the extension makes it harder to get in tight areas. Never remove this shield because it protects you and others from any flying objects that you may accidentally run over. It prevents you from breaking any windows if you were to run over a stone.

If you're not the do-it yourself type then you need to have a good mower shop that can do the routine maintenance. The oil needs to be changed, the tires may need air and filters need to be routinely replaced. It's important to grease the wheels at least once or twice each season. While the mower is in the shop be sure to have the blades sharpened, it's inexpensive and is certainly one of the most important ingredients to lawn success. Spray cooking oil on the bottom of the deck so the cut grass doesn't stick.

Garden Rebel Mowing Tips

1. Always use a sharp blade.

2. Never remove more than 1/2 of the grass blade at any mowing. About 1/3 rd. of the blade at a time is best.

3. Use a mulching mower.

4. Mow weeds before their seed heads develop.

5. Mow before you add extra seed to thicken up.

6. Mow before you spray liquid fertilizer.

7. Edge beds with an edger or hand trimmer.

8. Mow once a week in summer, however, twice a week in faster growing months, if you like.

9. Change the angle each time you mow.

10. Do not mow wet grass.

Mowing Heights

	SPRING	SUMMER	FALL	WINTER
Bahia	3-3 1/2"	4"	3-3 1/2"	3"
Bermuda	3/4"	1"	1"	3/4"
Centipede	3"	3-3 1/2"	3"	2-2 1/2"
Rye	3"			
St. Augustine	3"	3-3 1/2"	3"	2-2 1/2"
Zoysia	1-1 1/2"	1-2"	1-2"	1-2"

2

THE BUGS DON'T CARE

The bugs don't care about the beauty of your lawn, they never cared in the past and still won't care in the future. It's up to you to outsmart the bugs, and don't laugh, this sometimes can be quite a frustrating task. The bad thing is that you're really out numbered since their army numbers into the tens of thousands. The good thing is that your brain is thousands of times bigger and at times of war this fact becomes a great benefit.

Since there are as many bugs as there are stars in the sky I'm just going to list the ones that you are most likely to encounter. Get to know these bugs and how to get rid of them. Sooner or later they're bound to cross your path and your lawn.

By using the tonics in chapter nine as well as the ones in the Garden Rebel *Lawn Tonic* booklet, you will be able to stay ahead of the bugs.

Chinch Bugs

If you have a St. Augustine lawn you need to be aware of the damage that this guy can do. They can be found in other grasses but by far the St. Augustine is their favorite. Do your Garden Rebel QC (quality check) at least once a week in the spring, summer and fall. You'll know when you have them because yellow patches will occur and the grass will become thinner.

Feeding the grass too much with nitrogen fertilizers can actually help expand a chinch bug problem. If the grass stays wet for too long, it could weaken it and make it more susceptible to damage. Certain spots in the yard where there may be a lack of water, can encourage chinch bugs as they will always attack the weaker grass first. Grass is weakened over time if it is routinely mowed with a dull blade. The chinch bugs multiply and seem to know exactly where the weakest grass is. If you suspect that you could have chinch bugs in the lawn, try this:

To one gallon of water
3 Tbs. liquid detergent
3 Tbs. vegetable oil

Apply in the greener areas where the yellow borders the green. Soak the entire area and if they are there they will come toward the surface in less than ten minutes. Now, all you need to know is what they look like. The young ones could be red with a white stripe or black with white spots. They can grow up to 1/4 inch long. As they mature, they develop brown legs and the wings can be black, brown, or white. The white parts of the wings usually appear as patches.

Control

Ortho Dursban Lawn and Garden Insect Control
or
Ortho Dursban Lawn Insect Spray
Ortho Diazinon Soil and Turf Insect Control

A chinch bug lives only three months or so but before they go to the great chinch-bug cemetery they leave plenty of relatives behind to continue their lives' work. They are mostly active April through December but can occur in other months as well. Sometimes, there is a distinct "X" that can be seen on their backs.

There is a pair of false wings that never develop but aid them in hopping a little bit as they get older. If you ever get a really bad infestation, be sure to repeat a spraying about a week to ten days later. Then mark on the calender a date to repeat because new generations are probably on their way.

Lawn caterpillars

This bad-boy group includes sod webworms, cutworms, and armyworms. They especially love Bermuda grass and St. Augustine  varieties. Probably the one that does the most damage is the sod webworm. Eggs are deposited onto the blades and in seven days they hatch. In two weeks you begin to wonder why your grass looks so short even though you didn't mow it. They complete their vandalism in five to six weeks and can have several generations in a year.

Sod webworms do their eating at night. You can often find them in a curled shape, near the soil surface in the daytime. They can get up to 3/4 to one inch long and the bigger they are the more they eat and when they've finished they don't excuse themselves and don't expect a thank you. So you can recognize them, they have a brown head and spots with stiff hairs along a tan body. The adult is a moth that flies low always in a zig zag motion, it's wing span is about 1 inch.

Armyworms, cutworms, and grass loopers can grow one to two inches long.

Armyworms can feed in the day or night and can be black, brown, or green with yellowish stripes. The adult is a moth 1 to 1-1/2 inches with grey and white wings which flies at night. Luckily none of the worms eat the roots of any of your shrubs.

Cutworms grow one to two inches in length. The adult is a night flying moth. The moth is hard to control because new ones can fly in from next door. However, regular spraying with the tonics in my **Lawn Tonic** booklet will help keep populations lower. The caterpillar is brown to grey. They will eat at night or day and cut the blade at ground level. They will usually be curled when you find them. Before you spray you can use 1 cup of mild liquid detergent to your 20 gallon hose-end sprayer. Apply over the areas you intend to add an insecticide. About twenty minutes later you can apply the insecticide. A thick thatch layer is a good hiding place for caterpillars. If you have a thick thatch layer be sure to wear lawn spikes while cutting the lawn. Lawn spikes are specially designed sandals with long nails on the sole. They strap to your tennis shoes and after using them any insecticide can penetrate the thatch layer.

Control

-**Ortho** Sevin - dust or liquid
-**Ortho** Dursban Lawn Insect Spray
-**Ortho** Dursban Lawn and Garden Insect Control

Mole Crickets

There is more than one species of this guy and all of them have the same agenda--to destroy your lawn. The adults are about an inch long and they have well developed fore-legs which are adapted for tunneling. They kill the grass by eating it but also by creating air pockets with their tunneling which causes the roots to dry out and die. They can grow 1-1/2 to 2 inches long and their only redeeming quality is that they make great fishing bait.

They lay the majority of their eggs in early spring all the way up to mid summer. The earlier you apply the insecticide the better luck you'll have. If damage doesn't occur until late summer or fall, you need to be Johnny on the spot with your insecticidal weapons or you could loose your entire lawn. Make sure the lawn is moist before applying the insecticidal control.

There are three species of mole crickets and there is not a good one in the batch. One of the problems with mole crickets is that the Changa, Tawney and Southern, all vary in their life cycles, living about a year but they can destroy a lawn a lot sooner than that. A lot of "experts" and garden books will menton that mole crickets only attack Bahia. I can assure you this is not true. I have personally seen them in St. Augustine and Bermuda and have heard plenty of reports of them being in other grasses as well.

They live closer to the surface when they are young. In the spring as they get older they develop a tougher exoskeleton, making them harder to repel. In late summer and fall I classify them as "teenagers". They eat voraciously at this time and consequently do the most damage. They love to stay up late, eat all hours of the day and night and simply have no regard for your feelings. If allowed to continue their tirade, they'll eat you out of home and lawn, and basically take over.

In late fall and winter they will slow up on their eating habits and will tend to tunnel deeper in the soil making them harder to kill. Some have been known to tunnel two to three feet deep! Over the winter their wings will develop and early in the spring you'll see them flying around at night looking for a spouse to set up housekeeping with. Once they find Mr. or Mrs. Right, they do the hokey-pokey and soon lay eggs in any moist soil in your yard. Guess what? The process starts all over again.

Control

-**Ortho** Diazinon Soil and Turf Insect Control
-**Ortho** Dursban Lawn and Garden Insect Control

Billbug

You'll find these guys in almost any lawn that has been stressed from neglect. When you first see them you might think they're some kind of weird cockroach. The adult is a grey or brown weevil with a narrow head and wide body. They eat roots and multiply rapidly. Their favorite grass is Bermuda and zoysia but will get into the others as well. Their damage will be evident by brown or yellow circular patches that appear in the summer. Before spraying moisten the soil with a soapy water solution in your hose-end **sprayer, one cup of liquid detergent to 20 gallons of water.**

Control

-**Ortho** Dursban Lawn and Garden Insect Control

Grubs

Grubs have a yellow or brown head. They are the larvae stage of various beetles and they damage the lawn by eating the roots. They are white to grey and almost always curled. Like
 mole crickets they make great fishing bait. The damage to the grass will be in the form of irregular, yellow - brown areas that often are spongy.

If you continue to water and the grass wilts then inspect for grubs. Dig up some of the grass and sift through the soil. Usually you will find that the grass roots are completely chewed off. Before using a granular control moisten the soil with the soapy water solution. Immediately after using a granular, apply about a half inch of water.

Control

-**Ortho** Sevin Dust or liquid
-**Ortho** Dursban Lawn and Garden Insect Control
-**Ortho** Lawn Insect Spray
-**Ortho** Diazinon Soil and Turf Insect Control

Grasshopper

They have well adapted back legs that often keep them one step ahead of a big tennis shoe. The smaller they are the easier they are to kill. They do their damage by eating all parts of the blade. Once they are tired of eating grass they'll move onto what they think are bigger and better things, all the shrubs, trees and flowers in your yard! I want to stress to you that they absolutely must be controlled when they are small. As they age they develop a tough almost armor-like exoskeleton that has some ability to repel the full effects of an insecticide. Stepping on them with your tennis shoe works great but the big ones have been known to take the shoe away from you and chase you down the street.

Control

-**Ortho** Sevin liquid

31

Scale

This stationary insect is often mistaken for a disease because it has no head or legs. It simply looks like a tiny barnacle growing on the grass blade. They have a hard, sometimes, waxy shell that comes in a variety of colors. They often attack neglected grass, perhaps in lawns that were abandoned for a year or more. They kill the plant by sucking on its juices. The grass ultimately turns yellow and becomes very thin. After you spray, only one time, the scale is usually killed. However, the hard exo-skeleton does not fall off the blade the first few weeks after spraying. Touch the scales in two weeks and if they are dry and crispy, they're dead. If some new ones have hatched and are waxy in texture you will need to spray again. Do not walk on the grass until the insecticide is completely dry.

Control

-**Ortho** Dursban Lawn Insect Spray

Bermuda Grass Mite

This is an extremely serious insect that can kill the lawn very quickly. They only need seven days to complete their life cycle and multiply probably faster than other pests.

The damage will be evident because the blades will loose their color and almost always will curl. You are more apt to have mites in hot, dry weather and they attack neglected grass first. You need a magnifying glass or microscope to actually see them. Under magnification they have a yellow-white color and look like tiny worms.

Control

-**Ortho** Diazinon Soil and Turf Insect Control

33

Applying Insecticides

Always apply the insecticidal control exactly as it is labeled on the container. For years I have taught my radio and TV listeners to always read the label at least twice to make sure you don't miss anything. If there is something you are not perfectly clear about in any part of the directions then ask your garden manager or local county agent. Plant people are always willing to share their knowledge whenever they can.

Remember that insecticides are poisons and need to be respected as such. Always wear gloves and professional filtering masks can be purchased to avoid any possible odors. Wear long sleeves and never apply on a windy day. If the wind picks up while you are spraying, label your mixture and put up high where children can't reach it, then finish your spraying as soon as the wind stops. Put a label on it **Poison, DO NOT DRINK.**

If you can avoid it do not store insecticides that have already been mixed into solution. Only mix up the amount that you're going to need at any one time. All garden poisons, chemicals or naturals, should only be stored in a locked cabinet and should always be put on the highest shelves.

Hose-end Sprayer

I've always said that the hose-end sprayer is the second most important gardening tool; the shovel is the first. When applying, a fertilizer, insecticide or weed killer, I always visually mark out in my mind a 10 x 10 square area. With an even back and forth motion the solution should be applied, not missing any spots in the lawn. It is very important if you apply a weed killer that you do not get too close to your trees and shrubs or damage could occur. The Ortho Dial 'N Spray hose-end sprayer has an easy on-off trigger. You simply add the product, then set the dial and spray. There is no measuring or mixing needed. There are 14 different settings from 1 tsp. to 8 fl. oz. per gallon of spray. When you are finished, whatever you don't use, you can return to the original bottle.

GAL. SPRAYER

Every yard needs to have a Dial ' N Spray applicator because sooner or later the bugs will come and the weeds are never far behind. Besides a healthy lawn depends on you to feed it and some liquid fertilizers can be easily and efficiently applied this way.

Whirlybird Spreader

The Whirlybird Spreader has made a gardener's life so much easier and efficient. Lets say that you have an area that is small and just starting to become infested with insects. Now, get out the Whirlybird spreader and just treat the problem area. This spot treatment saves you a lot of time and I find it the best way to head off a problem before it can get out of hand. It has various settings and any Ortho granular insecticide can be applied through it. This applicator can not only be used for the lawn but it makes it easier to apply insecticides under shrubs and along the house as well.

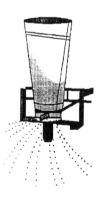

3

THE DISEASES DON'T CARE

Lawn diseases are only interested in one thing and it's not your garden party. I can't tell you, as a professional landscaper, TV host, radio host and teacher, how many times people have told me the following: "Garden Rebel, Garden Rebel, you'll never believe what happened. Our lawn used to be the prettiest one in the neighborhood. We went on vacation for two weeks and when we returned we almost didn't recognize the house. Most of the grass was dead!" Well, actually I do believe it because I know how fast lawn diseases spread. Folks, the minute you see a problem it needs to be spot treated. If you discover it once it has spread over the whole lawn, you especially need to treat it right away because if you procrastinate the next week you'll be going out in the lawn and will be laying new sod!

Diseases can spread due to many factors. Periods of heavy rains are one of the most common causes. They are also very active when the fog and dew is thick. Another common cause is setting the sprinkler timer to come on too often and not shutting it off when it rains. High humidity in the summer is yet another cause. Disease spores are spread through water droplets and as I've said so many times on my radio and TV shows, "It may be only a drop of water but to disease spores it might as well be the Atlantic, Pacific and all the other oceans combined."

Here's a list to memorize before applying any fungicide for common lawn diseases. If you have never had diseases in the lawn, consider yourself very lucky. If you happen to get any of them in the future, take swift action, never double dose fungicides, read the label at least **twice** and always store high on a shelf in a locked cabinet.

When applying fungicides:

1. Read label twice and follow exactly.
2. Do not mow grass immediately after you spray.
3. Do not water lawn immediately after applying (unless it is a special root drench) fungicide.
4. Do not allow any person or animal to walk on newly sprayed grass.
5. Never spray on a windy day.

Brown Patch

When it's hot and humid, be on the look out for it. Reduce your watering immediately if you get it in the lawn. In the summer months a darker ring along the perimeter of the patches is visible. The ring is harder to see in the winter and may not even be noticeable at all.

The bottom part of the blades rot and turn black or brown. Brown or tan strings of fungus are prevalent. This disease can kill grass blades in just a few hours.

The most common grasses that are affected are centipede and St. Augustine. You'll know something is going wrong because the blades will turn yellow before they die. The dead blades turn a red-brown color or a medium brown color.

The area usually is in the form of a rounded patch but often lawn mower blades spread the disease, and lawn areas can take on various dead shapes.

Do not fertilize your lawn when brown patch is evident and pick up and bag all lawn clippings to reduce the spread. It's bad, it's common and it must be stopped in its tracks immediately.

Anthracnose

I've seen this disease destroy a friend's centipede lawn. Reddish brown spots occur all over the blade and are surrounded by yellow areas.

This disease is more apt to occur in the spring but can occur anytime when rainfall is heavy. It's a bad scene as ugly as it sounds.

Dollar Spot

It's called dollar spot but don't let the name fool you. The spots can turn into large areas if they connect. Sandy soil that tends to be poorly fed is very susceptible as is grass with thick thatch.

The spots or lesions on the grass blades are irregularly shaped and are usually along the perimeter of the blades. It is sometimes mistaken for brown patch but dollar spot has distinct spots. The spots are tan and have a red-brown edge around them.

If you let this disease get out of hand, it will cost you alot more than a dollar to get it under control.

Fairy Ring

Fairy Ring fungi just may be the easiest disease to diagnose, because mushrooms or puff balls reproduce within the darker colored ring of the diseased grass. It can occur in the spring and summer and is known for coming back after you thought it was long gone. The rings can be very small to very large and anything in between.

Grey Leaf Spot

This is also an easy one to diagnose. The spots start out as small as pin heads and are green to brown in color. As the spots age they develop a grey velvet appearance, they then get bigger with brown or purple edges. The most active time is spring and summer.

Rhizoctonia Leaf Spot

This disease is closely related to brown patch and is often misdiagnosed as brown patch. It appears during the hot, humid summer months. Dead rings in the grass can be as small as a few inches and as large as several feet. The spots can occur on the blades as well as the sheath of the blades. The distinguishing fact is that the grass does not take on a decayed look like brown patch. Sometimes an occasional mushroom will appear but not in a circular ring pattern like Fairy Ring.

Slime Mold

Slime mold looks like creeping crud and gets a lot of people excited all for nothing. Actually, they are not even disease organisms. They are primitive fungi that do not harm the grass and come in a variety of colors. They develop a soot-like appearance on the blade. They may look ooky and gooky but they ain't spooky. There is no need to spray since they do not hurt the grass.

Control of Lawn Diseases

-**Ortho** Daconil 2787

4

THE WEEDS DON'T CARE EITHER

There is nothing that will make you want to put colored pebbles faster over the entire front yard than when the weeds get out of hand. The frustration builds and builds and some people never even want to walk out into their lawn to avoid coping with the problem. Well, if you don't already know it, you can run but you can't hide, there is no magic wand trick, you need to spray them, then follow through to make sure that the weeds are completely dead. Sometimes it takes two or three sprays to kill them all but I want to make it crystal clear that it will be your timing and persistence that will determine lawn success.

The best defense against weeds is a thick, healthy turf. When there are no open soil spots the weeds can never get a foot hold and never are able to multiply. Kill the weeds before they seed otherwise you have numerous generations all working toward the same goal--taking over your lawn.

Weeds occur when:

-lawn has been damaged from over
 fertilizing
-lawn stays too dry or too wet
-lawn is starved for food
-lawn becomes a high traffic area
-weeds are allowed to reach maturity
 and reseed
-soil is too compact for grass
-grass is damaged from mowing too low
-grass is damaged from insects
-grass is damaged from diseases
-new sod has weeds already

Herbicide

Herbicide is a fancy name for a weed killer. Like insecticides and fungicides you need to apply the proper type on the proper varieties. Never apply a herbicide under a desirable plant unless the label says that you can do so. A herbicide can be used to spot treat weeds to prevent them from multiplying. They can also be used in the Ortho hose-end sprayer when you have to spray large areas. When using your hose-end sprayer make sure the broad spray never goes into large patches of healthy grass or shrub beds.

Types of Weeds

Broad leaves - Interestingly enough, many broad leaf weeds have some very beautiful flowers and when in full bloom will even make you take a second look. We ultimately decide that they have to go. Make sure the weed killer that you get can be used on your specific type of grass. If you look at the veins of any broad leaf weeds you'll notice that they have a net veination on the bottom of their leaves. There are thousands of varieties including white clover, pusley, matchweed, spreading dayflower, creeping charlie, and spurge.

Grasses - Grassy weeds have stems that are hollow and their veins are parallel. Some examples of grassy weeds are goose grass, crabgrass, and torpedo grass. Some grow vertical, some horizontal, some both ways and all of them are bad. Choose a weed killer labeled for your specific type of grass that kills grassy weeds.

Sedges - the stems of sedges can be solid and round and some species have a triangular shaped stem. They are usually found in areas that tend to be a bit on the wet side.

Your garden shop will have specific brand formulations especially designed to kill sedge. Basagran is often used for yellow sedge and Image is used for purple sedge.

Types Of Weed Killers

Contact - This kind of herbicide affects only the portion of the weed that is sprayed. They are not translocated through the entire system of the plant. They do not kill underground bulbs, tubers, rhizomes or roots. Usually you will need to spray again to kill new growth that is revived from the base. Contact herbicides include Diquat, Finale and Basagran.

Systemic - These weed killers are absorbed throughout the entire plants and kill them over several days. Spray early in the morning so the warm sun can bake in all day. Systemic weed killers include Image, Banvel, 2,4-D and glyphosate (which is Roundup).

Selective - Most lawn herbicides fall into this category. They kill specific weeds but leave the grass in tack. Some varieties of grass may yellow a bit but will be revitalized in a few weeks.

Nonselective - These weed killers kill everything they touch. They are often used to spray on neglected lawns that have more weeds than grass. It's basically used when starting over. After everything is dead, the new lawn can be put into place. Glyphosate (Roundup) is a nonselective herbicide.

You Better Know How to Read When Choosing a Lawn Weed Killer

The garden shop will have a large selection of weed killers. You need to read the label carefully because different brands can only be used on **certain types** of grass. I have met and heard from many people who were in a hurry, just grabbed anything on the shelf, sprayed it on, and encountered the proverbial rude awakening. This disaster could occur with liquid and granular weed and feed products. If you don't understand something on the label ask the garden shop manager to help you out with information so that you choose the right product for your specific problem. New advanced formulations are always coming out and old standard formulations are often improved upon.

Precautions

As with insecticides and fungicides always read the label twice and never over dose because if you do you could end up killing more than the weeds. Do not spray on windy days and keep in a locked cabinet high on a shelf away from children and animals. Only mix up exactly what you need at the time you do your spraying.

Timing is Everything

Until you have a complete understanding of how important timing is you won't be able to get the weeds under control. For successful timing purposes there are premergence and postemergence control.

Premergence

If you intend to do any raking or dethatching you need to do it before you apply a premergence control.

They should be applied early in the spring and early in the fall. Make sure that you choose the right one for your specific lawn. Depending on the brand, premergence herbicides usually are affective for 1-1/2 to 3 months. Only use the amount suggested by the specific brand you choose as different companies recommended amounts will vary. You must apply the premergence control before the seasonal weeds germinate. Remember, never apply to young grass that is not established and do not apply if you just added fresh grass seed. If you wait too long before applying to established grass, the weeds develop and are not killed by a premergence. If you get your timing right and apply early in the spring and before the seeds germinate you have my permission to spend the rest of the summer patting yourself on the back!

Naturally, when all your neighbors ask; how in the world do you have such a perfect lawn? I expect you'll tell them, "I've been listening to that Garden Rebel guy again!"

Postemergence

As a general rule the younger a weed is, the more tender and more susceptible it is to a postemergence weed killer. Once they are old and toughened-up they are better able to resist the herbicide, and sometimes are not even affected.

Any weed is harder to kill if:

1. It has already gone to seed.

2. It is under water stress at the time of application.

3. It is mowed before applying the chemical.

Not all types of weeds are killed by all types of postemergence controls. On certain weeds you may have to do a follow up application. On other weeds you may have to follow up with a different product. Always double check to make sure that the weed killer you choose can be used on your specific type grass or your lawn will look like it's decorated for Halloween year round.

Weed and Feeds

I'm always asked if they're any good. You bet. They're great if your timing is great, which is early in the spring and early in the fall. You can't expect the weed and feed products to supply enough nutrients year round, so expect to do supplemental feedings with granular fertilizer, water soluble fertilizer, and the Garden Rebel Tonics. Read the label of any weed and feed products slowly and carefully because many types can severely damage trees, landscape shrubs and groundcovers if applied too close to them. Sometimes your fertilizer spreader can throw the product into the edge of the shrub planting bed and in just a few short weeks the plants on the perimeter start to turn yellow and drop leaves. If you have weeds in the shrub beds you can get specific premergence and postemergence products that are formulated especially for that type of application. The lawn controls are only for the lawns, no need to experiment with other areas, as the lawn formulations could definitely affect the shrubs, in a negative way.

After you use a weed and feed always store in a dry place. If stored by an open door or window, moisture could get into the bag and activate the ingredients.

5

CHOOSE THE GRASS THAT'S RIGHT FOR YOU

There are so many different types of grass species. There are probably varieties that you think are ugly and varieties that you think would be just perfect for your home. You need to do your homework to make sure that you choose the one that is appropriate for your amount of light, soil, water and maintenance lifestyle. This is how you do your homework to help you make a decision for which grass is best suited for your yard:

1.   Talk with two or three local nursery experts.
2.   Talk to the county agent in your area who specializes in lawns.

3. Only get advice from neighbors and brothers-in-law who have great looking lawns.
4. See if the library and bookstore have information for your specific area.
5. Talk with the grounds-maintenance manager at the best looking park in town.
6. See if the local Vo-Tech or Community College offers a local yard class.
7. Talk with the superintendent of your local botanical gardens.

While you are trying to formulate an opinion as to the best type for your yard. Keep in mind these important questions:

1. How much shade will it tolerate?
2. What bug problems will I have to cope with and which season do they appear?
3. Will it thrive in sandy soil?
4. Will it thrive in a lowland that may occasionally have extra moisture?
5. Will it tolerate drought?
6. Is an automatic sprinkler necessary?
7. How often should it be mowed?
8. Will it take heavy foot traffic?
9. Is it known for getting a lot of diseases?
10. How often does it need to be fed?

Types of Grass

Across the nation there are a wide variety of regional grasses. In this section I will briefly mention some of the popular Southern varieties.

St. Augustine Grass

Pros
- -many varieties to pick from
- -perhaps the most beautiful of all Southern grasses
- -solid thick turf
- -great salt tolerance
- -bitter blue and delmar tolerate shade
- -spreads fast by runners
- -adapts to wide range of soils
- -floratam is the Garden Rebel's choice

Cons
- -does better if irrigated
- -browns after frost
- -builds thatch fast
- -crawls over sidewalks and driveways if not maintained

There are several varieties of St. Augustine. As a general rule I am fond of the floratam variety, however there may be other types that are more appropriate for your specific location. Here's a few notes on some of the most popular.

Floratam

It does tolerate a little shade but dense shade will definitely thin it out and eventually it will die completely. It has fairly good drought tolerance when compared to other varieties of St. Augustine. In full sun it is very fast growing as well as thick. It has some resistance to chinch bugs. It's important to note that I said resistance and not chinch bug "proof." I like the dark green color and it continues to be the most popular of all the St. Augustine grasses. It is available at garden centers in the form of sod or plugs. Buy plugs only if they are dark green and do not have an abundance of yellow blades. If blades are too yellow the trays may have been stacked for too long or the plugs may have dried out.

Bitter Blue

This is the grass I grew up with. As I kid I maintained the yard and landscaped around the perimeter of a lush bitter blue lawn. Everyone always commented on how beautiful it was. We grew it under the dappled sunlight of live oak trees and although it was considered shade, was considered bright shade. It grows in full sun too and is especially nice for people who have both sun and bright shade in their lawn.

Seville

Like bitter blue, it is also ideal for the shade. It does not grow tall like bitter blue or floratam as it is a dwarf variety. If grown in full sun be aware that many people complain that it gets too thick and is like walking on pillows. Like any thick grass, it doesn't dry out as fast after watering or after a rain therefore, it has the potential to have diseases spring up. The minute you see even a small spot of disease, use Ortho's Daconil immediately. (Always follow label directions).

Seville is the favorite of some gardeners because it doesn't need mowing as often as many other varieties.

Delmar, Raleigh, Floralawn, and FX-10

Although I've heard plenty of wonderful reports from my radio and TV listeners about some of these, I have also heard plenty of disappointing comments from other growers. Probably delmar is the one I hear the best things about, especially from people who grow it in bright shade. The others really haven't caught on professionally. Whenever a new lawn variety comes out it is touted as the best thing since striped tooth paste. A lot of folks get excited, jump the gun and tear out their old lawn. Many people have been disappointed because sometimes they only perform well for one or two years then start to fall prey to a number of problems. A grass needs to be several years on the market in literally thousands of homes before it can be judged fairly. New varieties do not come along that often and I don't want to discourage you from investigating them further but be aware that when they first arrive there will always be a lot of hoopla that may not be warranted. A well designed marketing plan touting any new variety does not necessarily mean that it will be around in the years to come. Anybody can promise anything and until it has been around awhile be suspicious and cautious before spending your hard-earned money.

Bahia Grass

Pros

-irrigation not necessary
-deep root system
-withstands fair to high foot traffic
-few disease problems
-can be grown from seeds
-extremely cold tolerant

Cons

-it's the favorite food of mole crickets
-if not trimmed produces tall seedheads
-tough grass blades make you sharpen
 mower blades more often
-coarse texture
-not tolerant to salt spray
-spring and fall iron deficiencies
-hard to get thick

There are four main varieties of bahia sod. Of the four, Argentine is considered the best for lawn purposes.

Argentine

It is not as likely to get dollar spot disease that the others can sometimes get. Its blades are wider than Pensacola. It can grow dense and responds to fertilizer better than the others. It has excellent cold tolerance and has a good medium green color. I have ten acres of this grass and am very satisfied with one big exception, the mole crickets love it.

Common

This one has an open growth habit and is not recommended for a lawn. It is coarse in texture and its color is too light. Sometimes seed will be for sale of common at a give away price, but your response should be "thanks, but no thanks."

Paraguay

It is not as good a lawn grass as Argentine or Pensacola. It is susceptible to diseases and its cold tolerance tends to be low. The blades are very hairy which gives them a grey-green appearance. It tends to be stocky in its growth and is sometimes called Texas bahia.

Pensacola

This guy produces long ugly seedheads if it is not cut routinely. It tends to be tough and that qualifies it to be a good commercial roadside grass. It only needs water at first to become established. Seed is widely available and can be sprayed with a tea solution with your hose-end sprayer as soon as the seed is sown.

Bermuda Grass

Pros

-attractive color
-dense growth
-great salt tolerance
-great wear tolerance
-great drought tolerance
-chokes out weeds

Cons

-gets into planting beds
-nematodes often destroy it
-needs regular chemical applications
-very high maintenance
-browns in winter
-many insect and disease problems

Centipede Grass

Pros

-thrives in the poorest soils
-medium texture
-good shade tolerance
-establishes from seed
-good drought tolerance
-very low maintenance
-very dense
-low growing
-great cold tolerance

Cons

-attracts ring nematodes
-attracts ground pearl insects
-poor salt tolerance
-does not withstand foot traffic
-thick thatch if over fed
-iron deficiencies

Zoysia Grass

Pros

- good shade tolerance
- slow grower
- very dense
- very beautiful
- good wear resistance
- adapts to many soils
- does not have to be mowed often
- fun to pronounce

Cons

- seemingly takes forever to establish
- needs rich well-drained soil
- builds heavy thatch
- nematodes love it
- billbugs and diseases love it
- must use a reel mower
- shallow rooted

To Sod, To Plug, Or To Seed...

Sod

Sod has one major advantage. You can have no grass in the morning and a few hours later you can have an instant lawn. The ground needs to be raked level and any stones, large or small need to be removed. If there are any potholes or spots where water would sit after a long rain, they should be leveled or those spots will come back to haunt you. If you want to, you can buy large sod pieces and with a machete cut them into large quarters and space them to grow-in. New sod should be fed first with an organic blend of 50 / 50 Ironite and Milorganite. I also like to water it in with Ortho Up-Start. The first time you cut it you need to cut it high or you may cause a lot of damage to the lawn.

Never allow new turf to dry out or it will never become established. Check your sprinklers routinely to make sure all the corners are being covered. If you suspect that there are certain spots that are simply not getting enough water then you need to add a new sprinkler head or call your irrigation professional immediately because a brand new lawn is an expensive investment and you don't want to purchase any more sod than you have to.

Plugs

Lawn plugs have absolutely exploded in popularity in the last fifteen or so years. The reason is due to the simplicity and ease in which the homeowners can install them. They are purchased in shallow nursery trays that have individual compartments for each plug. Professionals can be hired to do the service for you and it usually ends up costing about half the price of sodding end to end. If you have a professional lawn service be sure to pay the extra money for them to put your lawn on a strict schedule to prevent weeds from invading, while the plugs are growing in. Over the years I've known plenty of folks who have big plans to do all the necessities themselves but somehow do not get the all important timing just right and weeds take over. Plugs are spaced, depending on the varieties and tend to grow in solid in seven months to one year from the planting date if well cared for.

Whenever a small spot in the grass has died from bugs or disease, plugs are such a simple and efficient way to mend the problem. This method is cost effective and popular.

Seed

Seed is for you folks who have more time than money. The most important thing I can tell you is to purchase fresh seeds and have the ground prepared and ready to go at a moment's notice. Next, watch the local weatherman daily and be ready to apply the seeds right before a soft gently falling rain that ideally would last one to three hours. Growing from seeds is the cheapest way to go but certainly has some potential problems. A variety of weed seeds can also blow onto the bare ground and they may germinate and guess what, your beautiful new seeds suddenly have evil competition. Once you realize this your heart sinks and you begin to think that you have a black cloud following you. If this happens to you then allow the weeds to grow up and before they can seed, zap them with a weed herbicide that is appropriate for your type of grass.

Seed is usually sold in bags of various sizes and some bags are puffed-up with a certain amount of air. Be wise, compare the pounds of seed per bag and do your arithmetic. You don't want to end up buying the brand in the biggest or prettiest bag!

pH

The pH is the alkalinity or acidity of the soil. It is important because it determines the lawns ability to absorb nutrients. If you suspect that you have a pH problem the first thing you should do is perform a test which can be sent to a local university through your local county agent. There is a nominal charge. Some garden centers offer the service as well. It is my opinion that unless you are a soil scientist you probably should consider having a lawn professional add the necessary nutrients to adjust the pH. If you make a mistake you could end up harming the soil for future growth.

Best pH Ranges For Lawn Grasses:

Bermuda	5.0 to 6.9
Centipede	5.0 to 5.9
Bahia	5.0 to 5.9
St. Augustine	6.0 to 6.9
Zoysia	6.0 to 6.9
Fescue	6.0 to 6.9

Feed Me

Different lawn grasses require different amounts of nutrients. A main factor that affects the amount of nutrients that are needed is the consistency of the soils. For example, sandy soils do not hold moisture or nutrients for very long and therefore would need more feeding than a rich, organic, well drained soil. Depending on the variety, you may need to feed a few to several times a year.

I am often asked which fertilizer formula is best. I think a variety of granular and water soluble is your best bet. If you vary the formulas and alternate granular and water soluble you will generally be better off with most grasses.

When a lawn is malnourished from lack of feeding it becomes thin and weak and may even die out in some areas.

A good routine to get into would be to supplement your granular food with 5 lbs. of magnesium sulfate (Epsom salts). Use 5 lbs. for every 50 lbs. of granular food. It should be thoroughly mixed in a wheelbarrow then shoveled to the fertilizer spreader. You'll notice a deeper richer green in less than 30 days in the warm months.

The brand of fertilizer that you choose will usually suggest how often it should be applied throughout the year.

Granular Fertilizers

These granular type fertilizers are what I call meat and potato foods. The higher the percentage of organic, the longer it will last as it will be a slower release. A higher percentage of organic will be less likely to burn the roots if accidentally overdosed.

When fertilizing any lawn the nutrients should be distributed as evenly as possible. For small courtyard areas or small townhouse or condominium yards an Ortho whirlybird spreader is the most efficient.

For larger yards the granular fertilizer is usually sold in twenty to fifty pound bags. It is best applied with a plastic fertilizer spreader. The spreader will have different settings and the bag of fertilizer will usually suggest the setting that the manufacturer recommends. The fertilizer should not be applied when the grass is stressed from drought.

Do not get too close to the shrub beds when feeding the lawn as many of the shrubs may not like the high nitrogen content that is usually associated with lawn fertilizers. Sometimes, the fertilizer is thrown into the bottom foliage of shrubs and some fertilizers have the potential to burn ornamental shrubs. If this happens wash off the foliage as soon as possible with a forceful spray of water.

If A Little is Good Alot Is Not Better

If you have never experienced the drama of overfeeding your lawn and killing it in a week or two, trust me, this is an experience you don't want to have. Over the years plenty of people have called me on the radio or TV to tell me the bad news that they killed their grass by being a little over zealous with fertilizer. We men seem to have the biggest problem with this issue. I tell my listeners that we men must carry a gene for overfeeding and not reading directions because I never get the frantic calls for help from women, who have killed their lawns. Remember to resist with every ounce of determination that you have when it comes to overdosing with fertilizer. It can burn the roots!

In regard to the various fertilizer formulas, try to alternate your formulas each time you feed the yard. A lawn's diet should be varied just like ours for the healthiest growth. As much as I love fettucini alfredo, if I had it every time I had dinner, sooner or later I might get tired of it! So it is with lawns and lawn food, alternate your formulas, use both granular and water soluble and over time you will help to create a lawn that is not only thick and green but will withstand bugs and diseases better. The old adage, you are what you eat certainly pertains to your lawn's health.

Thatch

Causes of thatch

1. Grass grows too fast.

2. Over feeding.

3. Infrequent mowing.

4. Soil not organic enough and thatch doesn't decay fast enough.

5. Over watering.

6. Failure to remove heavy grass clippings.

7. Very old lawn.

Why Thatch Is Something You Don't Want.

1. Causes roots to grow near soil surface or above surface.
2. Makes mowing harder.
3. Fertilizers do not penetrate.
4. Water does not penetrate.
5. Prevents good air movement at base of grass.
6. Promotes bugs and diseases.
7. Harder to walk on.

Controlling Thatch

Once thatch becomes too thick all you can do is rent a power dethatcher and boy, oh boy, does this tear up the lawn. Only do this as a last resort if bugs and diseases are taking over.

The control of thatch needs to start before it becomes a problem. This means control is needed even on young lawns.

The main goal to reduce thatch is to increase the microbial activity. A light liming of soils that are too acid will aid in the decomposition of thatch. Make sure that you do not over or under water. Always mow at the recommended rate to prevent excessive blades from building up. This is where a mulching mower is valuable.

A top dressing of a rich soil that is free of weed seeds is effective to reduce thatch, however it must be a light layer. Always do your top dressing in the warm months and given a choice, I prefer, early in the spring.

Raking

If you really want a workout get out in that lawn early one Saturday morning and rake up all the loose thatch. Make dozens of little piles and now you'll have the wonderful beginnings of a compost pile. Power rakes can be rented and do not cut the turf but remove any excess loose thatch.

Liquid tonic's to help reduce thatch (use on a regular basis)

1.   Commercial thatch products
2.   Liquid seaweed
3.   Fish emulsion
4.   Garden Rebel Tonic
       (To a 20 gallon, spray potential, hose end sprayer)

Fill half with beer and half with ammonia
add one cap dish detergent

alternate with

half soda pop (non-diet)
half beer
one cap dish detergent
This can be used as often as every two
weeks.

Feeding The Lawn With Your Hose-end Sprayer

The hose-end sprayer just may be one
of the most important gardening tools ever
created. Interestingly enough it is one of the
least used. When you buy your hose-end
sprayer, just don't use it once or twice then
retire it to the top shelf of the garden shed.
Get in the habit of using it routinely. Besides
water soluble fertilizer, any of my lawn tonics in
the Garden Rebel Lawn Tonic booklet can be
used throughout the year. In that booklet I
created a seasonal lawn tonic guide to keep
the grass looking it's best year round.

There are concentrate liquid fertilizers
that can be added to an Ortho hose-end
sprayer. There are also water soluble

fertilizers that need to have water added to a non-dialed sprayer. It's important to note that each brand of sprayer may have different directions for application and each brand of product will vary on the amounts of fertilizer to add. Once in awhile, water soluble fertilizer will clog the spray hose. If you add a golf ball, it will help agitate the mixture and keep it more soluble. Warm water will help dissolve any clumps.

After using any hose-end sprayer, be sure to wash it out before you put it away. You need to have two hose-end sprayers, one for fertilizer and one for weed killers. **Label the weed killer sprayer** with red paint so no one can accidentally use it to mix fertilizer. I've known several people over the years who just wash each sprayer before use but I rather be safe than sorry, no need to have even the slightest weed residue mix with the fertilizer.

One time a lady called me on the Garden Rebel radio show heard on 580 WDBO in Orlando, and relayed a sad story. It seems her husband picked up the wrong sprayer and sprayed weed killer on her blue ribbon rose bed. His response, "I never promised you a rose garden!" She didn't think that line was very funny. Her husband made up for it. On Valentine's day she received soil for a new rose bed, new roses she never had, a rose arbor and a white picket fence. I think he made up for it, don't you?

Your Lawn's Diet

A good lawn diet contains all the essential elements. It especially needs the primary nutrients, all the others are important too but in smaller doses.

Essential Elements

Primary Nutrients	Secondary Nutrients	Minor Nutrients
Nitrogen	Calcium	Iron
Phosphorus	Magnesium	Manganese
Potassium	Sulfur	Chlorine
		Molybdenum
		Copper
		Zinc
		Boron

Here are a few details on some of the most important:

Nitrogen:

1. Most important element for greening a lawn.
2. Never overdose or the lawn could end up dead.
3. Very mobile within the soil.

There are two basic groups when it comes to nitrogen, the water soluble type and the slow release type. Both have their advantages and disadvantages. I tend to like the granular organic types but it certainly isn't a problem if you alternate them.

Water Soluble Type:

* Less cost.
* Leach fast.
* Burns grass easily if grass is dry or if too much is put on.
* Almost immediately available to grass.
* Releases nutrients in all seasons.
* Applied usually at lower rates.

Slow Release Types:
* Releases slowly in cool weather.
* Applied at heavier rates.
* Rarely burn a lawn.
* Slow to leach.
* Cost more but lasts longer.

Phosphorus:
This is the element that is important for developing a strong, healthy, root system. Without good roots, the lawn can't survive times of drought and can never become thick and lush.

Potassium:
Potassium is like a stress tablet it prevents the turf from becoming more susceptible to diseases. It also builds its immune system to better resist extreme heat or cold.

Secondary Nutrients:

Calcium:

Calcium builds strong teeth in humans and it makes the grass grow stronger too. It's great to neutralize the problem of over feeding with the primary elements. If you have a dog that visits a favorite spot every day, by adding a light sprinkling of calcium it will help to neutralize the acid burn. You can also ask for garden gypsum at the garden center.

Magnesium:

Magnesium helps to green the grass. It aids in developing a better root system too. It can be purchased in garden centers as magnesium sulfate. It is the main nutrient in Epsom salts. I often supplement many organic fertilizers by adding 5 pounds per 50 pound bag of fertilizer. This is especially important for lawns in the south, but benefits all lawns.

Sulfur:

It's very important in regard to the proper pH of your soil. If the sulfur is not in the soil in the proper amounts the lawn will loose it's ability to take-in nutrients.

Minor Nutrients:

They're all needed but only in extremely small quantities. Many fertilizers have them already built-in. They will be listed along with all the other nutrients if they are in the fertilizer. The back of the bag will have a label that will list all the nutrients. I won't list the various details of all the minor nutrients because I don't want to bore you to death, however, just be aware that they are important.

'Don't forget
the iron on your lawn'

6

THE LAWN ALTERNATIVE

Groundcovers

There are certain spots in certain yards where grass simply won't grow. When people call me and exclaim, "Mr. Rebel, I put grass in this spot three times and it still keeps dying." To those folks I reply, remember what Henny Youngman's doctor said, "Don't do that!" So who ya gonna call? Groundcover busters! Lawns and shrubs are an integral part of a landscape design and both can be used when the situation calls for it. For example, some dense areas under trees will look unfinished and barren if not detailed with a groundcover. Here's some of my favorites for those shady spots in the southern part of the country:

English Ivy

There are many varieties. Some have small foliage, others large. The majority of them grow fast and even do well in areas where there are alot of roots. They need hand watering to get established.

Aztec Grass

This is not a grass but a liriope. It is certainly one of the groundcovers I use most in my residential designs. It is wonderful contrast in the landscape since it has a narrow white leaf. Grows in sun or shade.

Liriope 'Evergreen Giant'

It is the largest of all the many species of liriope! It tolerates a variety of soils and tolerates heavy root areas. This species may just be one of the most popular groundcovers in the entire south. I sometimes use it as the interior plant under trees and add a scalloped bed of its variegated sister, aztec grass around the perimeter.

Mondo Grass

No, it's not a real grass but it sure is pretty and never needs mowing every Saturday morning. It grows short, about six to eight inches and spreads by clumping. It can be spaced twelve to eighteen inches apart and eventually will grow-in solid. There is a dwarf variety that is exceptional.

AJuga

This guy grows very short, just a few inches, it has an attractive purple leaf and spreads. Ajuga grows in sun or shade and there is a variegated form that is stunning.

Asiatic Jasmine

There are many varieties of jasmine and I like all of them. It's a great plant to add on a steep slope where lawn grass is too dangerous to mow. It is fast growing and vinning so it tends to grow in edges of lawns or into shrubs. I think it's worth the extra maintenance because it's so tolerant in other aspects.

Fern

There are hundreds of varieties of fern. Most thrive in shade where the grass dies. The Boston types tend to be some of the more aggressive. Every year they should be thinned so that they don't choke themselves out.

Flax

This is a clumping groundcover that I introduced to the south a few years back. I love to use it in design because of its wide highly variegated color. It grows in full sun but thrives in the shade. If it ever gets scale insects spray with Malathion.

Juniper

It's wonderful for those full sun "hot spots" where grass will never grow. The low varieties like blue pacific and blue rug and procumbens 'nana' work great on slopes. Since they have needle-like foliage, they are great contrast in the design.

Lantana

It blooms most of the summer. It comes in yellow, yellow orange, purple, white, and a rose color. The rose variety is less common and called "confetti". They are poisonous so keep the animals and kids away.

Society Garlic

Beautiful lavender flowers that bloom in the summer and early fall. It even tolerates wet areas. It should be thinned every three years or so. It definitely smells like garlic so if you don't like the fragrance then don't plant it by the patio or bedroom windows. Adapts well to full sun or bright shade.

Daylilies

I love daylilies, you can never have too many of them. They need to be fed regularly for best blooms. Use ironite, bone meal, and blood meal, one handful per clump in late summer and fall. In the spring do the same thing every eight weeks or so but add one handful of bulb food per clump to help them bloom better. They come in every conceivable color and ask around if there is a daylily society in your area. Since they're so easy to grow and so beautiful they become addictive and you couldn't have a better hobby.

Heather

This bushy groundcover will bloom most of the year in sun or bright shade. When it gets too leggy, just cut it back and it will stay compact. Always prune heavily in the early spring and fertilize with azalea food. In design it tends to be overused so resist putting it everywhere you have an empty spot.

Here's a short list of good northern groundcovers if you live in the colder parts of the country.

Native Ferns   **Ajuga**
Periwinkle   **Baltic Ivy**
Purple Winter creeper **Evergreens**
Pachysandra   **Paxistima**
Iris (bulbs)   **Daylilies**

7

ANTS AND FLEAS IN THE LAWN

Ants are more troublesome year round than any pest I know of. They are especially prolific in the warmest months.

Sometimes people will tell me, "Oh Mr. Rebel, ants don't do that much damage, do we really need to kill them?" To that I reply, "You're kidding me, right?"   Red ants and fire ants can cause severe damage and pain to a toddler or even a dog or a cat. The poison is immediately taken into the blood stream and most people swell up with red welts. There is no question that it is a pain more severe than wasps stings. The pain can last for ten or more days and some people could be highly allergic and could need medical attention.

The ant that is the most aggressive, and the most prolific in numbers and the main one to be concerned about is the fire ant. They do not care which grass they build their ant condominiums in. The mounds may start out fairly small but can grow large in several days. If left undisturbed some mounds can grow to over 3 feet.

Besides getting into lawns, fire ants can build mounds around small seedlings, vegetable crops, fruit trees and ornamental landscape shrubs. They create air tunnels under the roots and can kill the plants.

Worker fire ants will look for food in the day and night and as incredible as it sounds can travel 100 feet from their nest. There are single-queen colonies and multiple-queen colonies, you don't want to have either one anywhere near your property.

After your first application of Fire Ant Killer, check the mound twenty-four hours later to see if there are any survivors. If so, a second application will get them.

Control

Ant-Stop™ Orthene Fire Ant Killer
or
Fire Ant Killer Granules

Sugar Ants

I can't tell you how many times people have had these guys in the house and plenty of times the ants almost won! Spray inside the house along the baseboards and behind every nook and cranny you can reach. They are always looking for sweets so stop eating in bed. These ants can bite but it isn't a very hard sting.

Control

Ant-Stop™ Ant Killer Spray (aerosol)
Ant-Stop™ Ant Killer (hand sprayer)
Ant-Stop™ Ant Killer Bait

Fleas

They multiply the fastest during hot humid weather. They jump on humans and are brought indoors on shoes and pant legs. Of course dogs and cats bring them inside as well. If you ever get them in the house, they can live inside all winter where its warm and comfortable. They feed on blood and can complete their life cycle in several weeks but under just the right conditions can live up to two years.

Control

Flea-B-Gon Total Flea Killer Indoor Fogger
Flea-B-Gon Total Flea Killer Indoor Spray
Flea-B-Gon Flea & Tick Killer Outdoor Spray
Flea-B-Gon Outdoor Flea and Tick Killer
Fleanix Natural Indoor Flea Killer
Dursban
　　　Ready Spray Outdoor Flea & Tick Killer
Home Defense Indoor & Outdoor Insect
　　　Killer
Home Defense Flying & Crawling Insect
　　　Killer
Home Defense Hi Power Indoor Insect
　　　Fogger

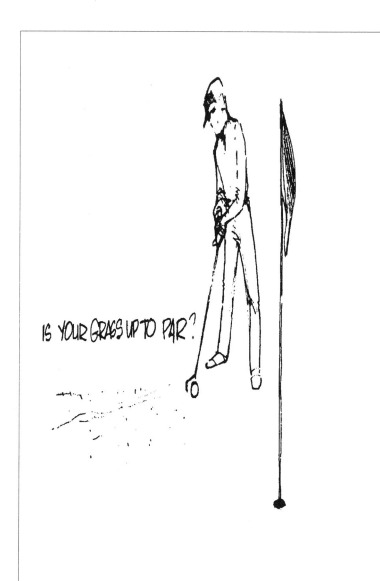

IS YOUR GRASS UP TO PAR?

8

SELECTING A LAWN MAINTENANCE COMPANY

There seems to be two types of homeowners when it comes to having a professional lawn service: those who complain, and those who complain and take action. Everyday people complain to me about what their lawn professional doesn't do. They don't weed, they don't always cut on time, they mow when the grass is wet and the list goes on. Often I will ask, "How long have you had this lawn man?" The answer is often like, "Oh, I guess it's going on three years now. No, Mr. Rebel, I think it's even longer than that." Well, let me tell you how I would handle the situation:

I would give them a fair chance. Any good professional can get the lawn in shape in six months or less. If you are paying your hard earned money for them to kill ants, spray for diseases and mow then I would expect the lawn to be in good shape all the time. If they are only paid to mow then make it crystal clear to them to leave you a note on the front door if they find that insects or diseases are beginning to take over. I don't care how friendly they are or about they're numerous excuses of why they can't get the yard in shape. Either they can do the work and improve the yard or they can't. It is up to you to not sign long term contracts. I'll say it again six months is enough for anyone to get the yard in shape. The more they give you excuses as to why something can't be done the brighter your inner little light bulb should shine as a warning to start looking for a new company.

It is the opinion of many homeowners I meet that a good lawn person is hard to find. Yes, I agree this is true. But, I can assure you that there are plenty of conscientious professionals who really take pride in their work and can bond with your yard.

Bonding

If your lawn professional does not bond with your yard it's a lost cause. Their ego must be totally involved with your lawn. It should be a source of pride with them since they are the ones that determine its beauty. If a large company has a different technician every time they come to do work then don't expect to have as great of success. Some companies hire people with little or no actual field experience. A compliment for good work goes a long way with anyone who works for you. It's important that you personally talk to them as often as you can on their weekly visits. If they're doing a great job, let them know how much you appreciate it. Most of them are hard working family people who are honest and want to please.

If you work during the day and cannot meet with them, then occasionally leave notes for them on the door and leave a message on their answering machine. This reminds them that you notice their work and care about your lawn. If you have a hard time meeting with them then check your calendar and set up a time to review the work you are paying them for and put the date you can meet them on a piece of stationary when you mail in their check. Put your home phone number on the paper and ask them to confirm with you the same evening that they receive your request.

If you have any kind of problem with the technician or the quality of work, then call a meeting with the supervisor. If the company you have is spraying for weeds and if the lawn still has weeds after several months then this is what you ask the supervisor face to face:

1.) What type of weeds do I have?
2.) How long will it take to eradicate them?

You absolutely, positively must get a date from the supervisor as to when you will have positive results. Now, make a note of the date and set up a specific time when you will have your follow up visit with the supervisor. Be concerned and be firm and business-like. This lawn is your investment and you can still be friendly and get the desired results. Lawn professionals deal with a lot of people day in and day out and they have to know that you are a homeowner that cares. If you don't let them know how much you care then you can't expect them to care. Remember, they have to bond with your yard. After you smile and thank them and shake their hand you're still not finished. Now, while you are thinking of it go inside and draft a friendly note something similar to:

Dear John,

Thank you for meeting me today. As you are aware, our lawn is very important to us. (As well as the neighbors, ha, ha). Our lawn is a major investment so if there is anything that we ever need to be aware of please call us at home or at work so bugs, diseases, or weed problems never take hold.

I look forward to talking to you again on June 1st. to see the results.

Once again thank you for maintaining our lawn and we look forward to telling our neighbors about your professional work.

Sincerely,
Mr. and Mrs. Green Grass

Selecting A Company

If price is going to be your sole reason for hiring a lawn professional then don't expect to get the best service for the least amount of money. The mow and blow lawn service is scheduled too tightly in my opinion and seems to spend less time each time they arrive. The best way to select a company is the old fashioned way, ask a neighbor. Take a close look at who has the best looking lawn on the street. Be bold, go introduce yourself and compliment their beautiful yard and let them know you're in need of a good lawn service and ask if they are satisfied with the company that they have.

Once you meet the person who is representing the lawn service:

1. Ask for references and call them!
2. How long have they been in business?
3. Will the same technician be taking care of my lawn each time?
4. How often do they fertilize?
5. Will they let me know the days and seasons they fertilize?
6. How much training does the technician have? (The company is only as good as the person that takes care of your lawn.)
7. Do they require a contract? (If they want more than six months, politely explain that you are only willing to do six months.)
8. Do they use both liquid and dry fertilizers?
9. Will they come the same day each time?
10. If it rains on the day they are scheduled when do they reschedule to do the work? (The next day, first thing in the morning is best.)

Garden Rebel Tip #1
Always ask your lawn company to spray your yard early in the morning-- afternoon service has the potential to be rushed if the technician gets behind schedule.

Garden Rebel Tip #2
Do not sign any contract without reading the fine print. If there is something that you do not agree with then you can cross it out, initial the change and mail the contract to the office. Do not sign any contract while the technician waits for you to review it. Take your time, rushing leads to mistakes.

Garden Rebel Tip #3
Memorize tip #1 and #2.

'HOOKED ON TONICS'

9

EVERY LAWN LOVES A TONIC

A tonic is just that, an energy vitamin, that does make a noticeable difference. If you could see the thousands of complimentary letters I receive each year you would be shocked.

In addition to your regular lawn feeding with liquid and dry fertilizer a tonic can be just the thing to help create the picture perfect lawn. These tonics can be used from one to several times each season. If you're ambitious and want to apply the tonics every two weeks it wouldn't be too much. They should always be used to water-in your granular fertilizer throughout the year. All of these tonics are for a 20 gallon spray potential hose-end sprayer, these tonics are designed for the non-dial sprayer. Be sure to shake the sprayer well before applying to the lawn. Here's one for each season.

Spring

To a 20 gallon spray potential hose-end sprayer:

> 2 cups milk
> 1 cup non diet cola
> 1/2 cup Dursban
> 1/2 cup Daconil

Summer

To a 20 gallon spray potential hose-end sprayer:

> 1 cup beer
> 2 cups lemon scented ammonia
> 1/2 cup liquid Dursban
> 1/2 cup liquid detergent

Fall

To a 20 gallon spray potential hose-end sprayer:

> 2 cups ammonia
> 1 cup beer
> 1/2 cup liquid detergent
> 1/2 cup Daconil

Winter

To a 20 gallon spray potential hose-end sprayer:

> 2 cups ammonia
> 1 cup beer
> 1/2 cup Diazinon (liquid)
> 1/2 cup liquid detergent

These tonics can really make a positive difference in your lawn. Lawns continually seem to be the biggest source of frustration to gardeners all over the world so the idea is that the tonics will help give you that winning edge.

For you folks that really get into the care of your lawn, you will be pleasantly surprised.

A perfect lawn has become the "goal" of so many gardeners. Allow me to fill you in on just a little "lawn reality."

Garden Rebel Lawn Reality

1. The lawn is rarely perfect and if it ever gets to the point of being perfect it will remain that way for approximately 15 minutes.

2. The lawn always grows faster than you can mow it.

3. It starts to die the minute you pull out of the driveway on your way to a vacation.

4. If you could get the grass to grow as well as the weeds, you would make a million bucks.

5. After you spray for insects you soon discover that it was a fungus problem.

6. It always rains right after you spray.

7. The mower repair shops are always their busiest when you need the mower the most.

8. The insects always kill the grass in the most visible spot.

9. It always rains on the day it was your only time to mow for two weeks.

10. Your neighbors on each side never mow on the same day you do.

Garden Rebel Lawn Tips

1. When you're granular fertilizing your lawn put flour in your spreader with your fertilizer. The flour will leave a white film on the grass and this will show you where you have missed fertilizing as you walk down each row.

2. Remember routine is the key to gardening. Routine watering, routine feeding, routine checking and spraying for diseases.

3. Spray Round-up once a month on weeds under trees to control.

4. To "break-down" your compost pile apply 6-6-6 and beer once a month. Also sprinkle Drain-zyme to stimulate the organisms that break down the compost.

5. When fertilizing follow directions. You know the saying, "a little is good, therefore a lot is better." This saying does not apply to fertilizing.

6. When weeding your garden give names and faces to the weeds of people you don't like and beat the daylights out of the weeds against the sidewalk as you shake off all the soil from the roots. This will drain you of all the hostilities then you can go take on the day.

7. Only remove about 1/3rd of the blade when mowing. If you remove more you're taking away the lawns ability to manufacture food for itself.

8. Mow in the mid to late morning and evening hours, why make it harder on yourself in the heat of the day?

9. Lawn spike sandals can be used to aerate any lawn. Older lawns especially become too compact over time and the grass can thin. They can be purchased for about $20.00 and should always be used before you feed.

10. Do not mow too early in the morning as the dew on the blade will not allow a clean, even cut.

11. If you mow when the gnats are out then

wear a wide brimmed hat and tape a piece of fabric softener on the hat to repel the gnats.

12. Use a mulching mower and your thatch will not build as quickly.

13. Water your lawn seeds with a tea solution in your hose-end sprayer; they'll germinate faster.

14. When applying seed in your spreader apply about half in one direction and half in the opposite to get the best distribution.

15. As a special tonic occasionally spray fish emulsion with your hose-end sprayer. It doesn't smell great but the lawn will be green.

16. Try to granular fertilize right before a rain and let Mom Nature be your co-worker.

17. If you just can't get into edging with a power edger then just spray a one inch strip of Round-Up along the perimeter of the shrub beds, once a month.

18. If you have weeds in the lawn, be sure to always mow before the seed heads have a chance to fully develop.

19. If you don't have the time to maintain your lawn properly, then hire a professional.

Someone has to keep your property value up.

20. When adding winter rye grass to your existing lawn add 7 to 10 pounds per 1,000 square feet.

21. Remember to use both liquid and dry fertilizers for a healthy lawn.

22. Get the Garden Rebel Tonic booklet, your lawn will thank you for it.

23. Always mow with a sharp blade. A dull blade tears the grass and the tips will yellow and then turn brown.

24. Add new lawn plugs as soon as possible when a spot dies out so weeds don't grab that spot first!

25. Maintain your mower like you do your car. Give it regular check-ups. Good machinery is too expensive to buy twice!

26. Pay for lawn service when the job is completed, never in advance.

27. If weeds continually crawl over from your neighbor's lawn then add a friendly hedge. A friendly hedge stays less than 4 feet. It will act as a barrier to you lawn.

GIVE ME A CHANCE
AND I'LL MAKE A MOUNTAIN OUT OF A
MOLEHILL.

10

Moles: They're So Bad, They Get Their Own Chapter

There is no question that moles are the most frustrating pest. I would rather have a dozen insects than two moles tearing up the lawn. They can travel about twelve feet an hour and it doesn't take long before the lawn gets so soft that you could easily sprain an ankle. They eat insects so if you can diminish the amount of insects in the lawn they will no longer find your yard to be their favorite smorgasbord. Their favorite food is cutworms and grubs and while they're looking for them they have no interest in being neat and organized.

Because their damage happens so suddenly most people are shocked and think that an entire family of moles has set up housekeeping. This is usually not the case.

All the damage is caused by one or two moles. Moles make two main types of tunnels. The surface tunnels are the ones that you see on top of the ground. These are the ones they use when they are actively looking for insects. They retrace their runs or tunnels about three to five times per day. They tend to use those long hallways about 11:00 A.M. and again between 4:00 P.M. and 6:00 P.M. They also use them all night long. The deeper tunnels can be one to two feet and that's where they hang out all winter. I've often wondered what it would be like if we could see a cross section of their tunnels. I wonder if they have little couches and little kitchens and mini refrigerators where they can store excess bugs. They are sightless but it doesn't deter them from finding plenty of food. They have strong forelegs and claw-like hands for digging. They also have long pointy noses.

There are various ways to get rid of them and you absolutely must not give up. Keep trying until you come across the one that works best for you. Any type of deterrent that you put down into their tunnels must be inserted while you wear plastic gloves. Do not allow the human scent to get onto whatever it is that you are putting into the tunnel. Here's the check list and if you discover any others that are worthwhile be sure to let me know. Those darn moles are getting smarter all the time and it's extremely embarrassing for any of us to admit that we have been outsmarted by a mole.

Traps:

Traps can be purchased at the garden center. Moles are shrewd and it takes a lot of patience to catch them. Often they will notice that a tunnel has been disturbed and tunnel around it. I've known people who said that traps didn't work then finally on their seventh or eighth try they caught one. If you ever see a mole, **never** touch it as they carry diseases and have the ability to do a severe scratch with their sharp claws. Some states may require a permit to trap.

Gas:

Special mole gas cartridges are available and plenty of people have called me to tell me that they had great luck with them. You can insert them at the opening of the tunnel. You'll know where the opening is because the tunnel will be raised in a little pyramid in one particular spot. Read directions carefully and keep well away from children.

Poison Peanuts:

These are sold in the garden center. Be sure to read the label exactly and wear plastic gloves when inserting them. They can be poisonous to other animals and children so be cautious when you use them and the unused portion should have the top tightened and placed on your highest garden shelf.

Pinwheel Daisies:

A pinwheel daisy is a simple little plastic flower on a two foot metal stick. As the wind blows it sends a vibration into the tunnel, just driving the moles crazy. Sometimes they get so crazy that they tunnel even faster and harder trying to get away from the vibration. This of course makes even more tunnels, but if they can tunnel just far enough to the neighbors' properties you'll be able to start closing their playground at your house.

Soda Pop Bottles:

This is what all the old timers used before all the other stuff was around. You simply bury the bottles into the tunnel with only the neck sticking up. When the wind blows in a particular direction a whistling vibration is permeated throughout the ground and it shoos them off with a headache. Be sure to remove the bottles before you mow.

Mothballs:

This is the stuff that gives them one heck of a stomach ache. Once again wearing the plastic gloves, drop flaked naphthalene moth crystals every four to six feet. It's important to always step on the tunnels the day before you apply this so that you can see which tunnels they are using at the time. Simply take a stick and make an insertion into the tunnel, then drop the mothballs or crystals into the holes, cover the holes and hope for the best.

Human Hair:

I think that it's hilarious that moles think our hair is obnoxious. They act like they wouldn't touch us with a ten foot pole! This is what you do. Wearing plastic gloves take as many clumps of hair as you can get and put them down into their runs. Bring a bag to your local barber I'm sure he'll be glad to give you plenty of hair.

Sometimes they will actually push it up as if to say, "I don't think so." Other times they just move onto a less intimidating environment.

Chocolate Laxative:

You know the saying, "everybody loves chocolate." This is certainly true to moles. They go after the chocolate covered laxatives thinking that they are free candy bars. Later that night, after eating a little solid food, like a few grubs or beetles it suddenly happens. That "happening" is very uncomfortable for them as well as their friends that use the same tunnels. Let's just say that it gives new meaning to the term mole runs.

Red and Black Pepper and Onion:

Mix up the two hottest peppers you can find and some onions. Place this into the tunnel and water just a little bit. If you are lucky they won't use it to prepare a gourmet dish. Red pepper can also be sprinkled at the entrance of a tunnel.

Hot Sauce, Detergent and Mothballs

Mix equal parts of hot sauce, detergent and mothballs and water lightly . Oh man, that's going to taste bad.

Garlic and Mothballs:

Mix equal parts of garlic and mothballs and insert into the tunnels. Even if their favorite food is Italian they won't like the mothballs mixed in. Just in case you're wondering they don't use the recipe as a salsa to dip the grubs into.

Hair / Bloodmeal Combo Plate:

Mix equal amounts of hair (can be human or dog) with bloodmeal and place in the tunnel. Be sure to water-in.

Hot Sauce / Urine Mix:

I'll leave out the details of assembling your materials but I'm sure you'll figure it out. Be sure to always mix-up what you intend to use at any one time. If the neighbors actually see you pouring what looks like bloody urine on your grass just tell them you've been real sick.

Castor Bean:

Castor beans are poisonous to moles so place as many beans as you can deep into the tunnels every two to four feet. Do not leave these beans around for children to find.

Camphor and Castor Oil:
Take several sprigs of camphor and boil them in a quart of hot water, now add two tablespoons of detergent and six tablespoons castor oil. Shake and pour into the entrance of the tunnel.

Kitty Litter:
Bury the kitty litter that has already been used by the cat in as many places in the tunnels that you can. Now, water in.

Soap and Mothballs:
Shave soap that you have and place into the mole's tunnel. Every time you water or it rains the soap is activated and works even better. I know of a couple who saves all of the small soaps from their hotel rooms while on vacation and use them for this purpose.

Soap / Castor Oil & Vegetable Oil:

Pour on top of the tunnels.
To one gallon of water:
  6 Tbs. liquid detergent
  6 Tbs. castor oil
  6 Tbs. vegetable oil

This can be made even more effective by slicing several garlic cloves and an onion and letting the mixture sit overnight.

Chewing Gum:

While wearing gloves peel the wrappers away from the sticks of gum. Now insert one stick every four to five feet in the newest tunnels.

Cigarette Butts:

Collect old cigarette butts and place them deep into the tunnels. Go out at night with a flashlight and if you see the mole smoking the cigarette butt and chewing gum at the same time you'll know that you need to try a different method.

Other Books by the
Garden Rebel

Robert Vincent Sims

Azaleas, Camellias & Gardenias

Answers To The Most Popular Questions

Groundcovers & Vines

Do It Yourself Landscape

Lawn Tonics

Old Fashioned Recipes

Recipes II

Roses

Shrubs

Vegetables *Naturally*

Vegetables "Bug Off"

LIFTING THE MIND FOG

ROBERT VINCENT SIMS

NEW

Look for the Garden Rebel's popular
motivational book *Lifting The Mind Fog*.
It's 130 inspirational pages that you'll
want to read and reread. It also makes a
fantastic gift for friends and families who
have everything!

GARDEN REBEL tm **BOOKS**